Original title:
Golden Lights, Frosty Mornings

Copyright © 2024 Creative Arts Management OÜ
All rights reserved.

Author: Hugo Fitzgerald
ISBN HARDBACK: 978-9916-90-902-7
ISBN PAPERBACK: 978-9916-90-903-4

A Luminous Chill

The sun peeks out, a lazy pup,
Sipping cocoa from a golden cup.
It giggles bright on icy ground,
While snowmen wear their hats all brown.

Penguins slide and twirl with glee,
Wearing shades by the frosty tree.
Snowflakes dance and have a ball,
While snowballs bounce and make us fall.

Frosted Sunlit Threads

A shiver wraps the morning tight,
But sunshine winks, oh what a sight!
Icicles giggle, they jingle and sway,
As squirrels plan mischief for the day.

The trees are dressed in sparkling lace,
While rabbits hop with a breakfast face.
Chasing shadows, they skitter and dash,
Accidental leaps causing a splash!

Winterscape of Glowing Beauty

The world glimmers, a frosty prank,
With snowflakes swirling in a merry rank.
Santa's sleigh seems stuck on a wire,
While reindeer munch on cookie fire.

Hot cocoa spills and giggles burst,
As penguins dance, oh how they thirst!
For marshmallows that float like snow,
Their attempts to catch them steal the show.

Ray-tingled Frost

Sunbeams stretch and start to tease,
As we slip on coats with such a breeze.
Frosted grass tickles our feet,
As we fumble, trying to retain our seat.

Giggling children chase the sun,
Wearing mittens in a playful run.
Oh, what a sight, what a splendid spree,
Can anyone beat this frosty jubilee?

Illuminated Silence of Dawn

In the morn when the sun gets shy,
The cat slips past with a sleepy sigh.
Pajamas dance in a whirlwind spin,
As coffee brews, let the chaos begin.

Birds gossip like they're in a club,
Squirrels plotting to steal the grub.
I trip on my shoelaces, oh what a sight,
But laugh it off with pure delight.

The toast pops up, it's a little burnt,
Like my plans—oh how they always turned!
Yet, the glow of dawn warms every fail,
As outside, frost leaves a cool trail.

So here we stand, in this lovely mess,
Life's one big joke—don't you agree, yes?
With hugs and chuckles, we seize the day,
While the sun finally joins the fray.

Soft Aureate Shivers

When the chill makes your nose turn red,
And your socks are mismatched, as I said.
A soft gleam sneaks through the frosty air,
Whispers of warmth that lift the despair.

Hot chocolate spills—oops, what a drench,
Laughter erupts, oh no, not the wrench!
As we bundle up, each layer clings tight,
With hats that defy gravity's sight.

The dog chases snowflakes, oh what a fool,
Tripping on ice like he's lost in a duel.
We share our stories while the world glows,
Amidst the giggles, the friendship just grows.

We'll dance in the frost, the world feels divine,
In this frosty set, we're simply so fine.
Life's too short for a gloomy parade,
So let's bask in the smiles we've made.

Sunbeams on a Frozen Canvas

On frosty fields, the sun does play,
Dancing beams chase chilly blues away.
Snowmen chuckle, hats askew,
With carrot noses wearing dew.

Oh, what's that slip? A clumsy pout!
Watch the dog, he's in a spout!
Paws like ice, a twirl, a spin,
Now he's stuck—let's dig him in!

Crystalline Radiance

Sparkling glints on rooftops bright,
Like little disco balls in flight.
A squirrel's acorn goes astray,
He chases it in wild ballet!

Beneath the snow, a hidden prize,
A cold-kissed donut, what a surprise!
Frosty bites and giggles ring,
Oh, winter's joy makes my heart sing!

Morning's Silken Glimmer

Mornings shimmer, just like jelly,
Frosty toes make everyone smelly.
Jumping joy—a snowball fight,
But oops! I missed; that's not polite!

A plump snowman waves hello,
With frosty gloves, he steals the show.
Carrot's lost, he needs some help,
In this winter's wacky yelp!

Chilled Sunfire

The sun peeks out, a playful tease,
While kids are rolling in the freeze.
Laughter echoes, snowflakes dance,
A penguin slip—who took the chance?

A frosty mug of cocoa dreams,
Filled with giggles, whipped-cream streams.
With every laugh, the warmth ignites,
In this silly world, we take flight!

Radiant Thaw

The sun peeks out, a wink so bright,
The snowmen dance, with pure delight.
Penguins sliding, in a clumsy race,
While squirrels giggle, a wild embrace.

Hot cocoa spills on pants with glee,
The dogs are playing, endlessly.
Winter's charm a jolly prank,
As ice melts down, a slippery plank.

Winter's Gilded Touch

The trees are dressed in sparkly fluff,
Children pretend, they're made of tough.
One brave lad throws a snowball high,
It lands right back, oh my, oh my!

Foggy breath forms a giggle spell,
While parkas clash, we laugh so well.
Snowflakes fall, a soft confetti,
Our noses red, but hearts are ready.

Morning's Sparkling Veil

A blanket white, it glistens bright,
The cat jumps out with all its might.
Coffee brews with a frosty twist,
As sugar lumps give it a wisp.

The laughter rises with chilly breath,
As frostbite threatens, the cold has heft.
We slip and slide, the ice a tease,
Calls for help sound like merry pleas.

Shards of Light on Icy Ground

Rays of sun through frosty haze,
A cat on a ledge, in a daze.
The mailman slips, it's quite a joke,
While we sip tea, and giggle, poke.

Snowballs fly in a flurry mad,
A snow angel screams, 'I'm not that bad!'
With each bright shard, the moment's clear,
Amid winter's chill, we spread the cheer.

Frosty Radiance

The sun sneezed bright on icy chills,
While snowmen danced on frosted hills.
A penguin slipped on banana peels,
And giggled loud with frosty squeals.

Chasing shadows, we pranced with glee,
Building castles by the frosty tree.
Hot cocoa dreams in a chilly breeze,
Life's a joke that tickles with ease.

The Warmth of Crisp Beginnings

Morning dew like jellybeans,
We stumbled through the frosty scenes.
A squirrel laughed, dropped acorn snacks,
And off we went on snowy tracks.

The sun's warm grin on frozen toes,
We'd slip and slide, wear funny clothes.
Ice skates squeaked like a doggone tune,
As we twirled and whirled like a cartoon.

Sunlit Frost

Candles flicker in bright array,
While we figure out how to play.
A snowball fight becomes a mess,
Our faces wrap in winter's stress.

With giggles echoing off the trees,
We race away, dodging the freeze.
Frosty breath forms goofy shapes,
As laughter fills the chilly drapes.

Wintry Gold

In a world of giggles and frosty breath,
We prance with joy, defying death.
A snowflake flops on a moonlit grin,
From the trees, a raccoon calls, 'Let's begin!'

Sipping tea with marshmallows afloat,
We chat with the frost in our silly coats.
Laughter dances like the morning sun,
As we toast to winters full of fun.

The Soft Touch of Dawn

The sun yawns bright, a sleepy face,
As frost slips from the grass with grace.
A rooster crows, his morning call,
I swear he thinks he rules us all.

The coffee brews, it hisses loud,
While neighbors skulk, all wrapped like shrouds.
A cat darts past, its tail a blur,
Should've started today with a purr.

Entwined in Frost and Warmth.

I stepped outside, what a wild sight,
My breath appeared like ghosts in flight.
The ground was white, a frosty quilt,
With every step, I danced and spilt.

My fingers numb, I slipped a bit,
Chasing a squirrel, I fell and split.
Laughter echoed in the chilly air,
Next time I'll wear boots, if I dare!

Dawn's Gilded Whisper

The sunrise flirts with a cheeky grin,
Waking up birds for a morning din.
A cat on a fence, oh what a sight,
Pretending to catch all the sun's light.

Snowflakes twirl like a dance on ice,
But my hot cocoa is way too nice.
Each sip brings warmth, but oh dear me,
This mug is slipping, just wait and see!

Icy Veils of Dawn

Frosty windows, like lacy art,
Nature's humor, playing a part.
The jogger slips, with legs akimbo,
Laughing louder than a friendly bimbo.

Birds in scarves, chirping a tune,
Reminding us spring will be here soon.
With each chilly giggle we share today,
We'll cherish the freeze, then melt it away!

Sunlit Frost's Dance

In the morning glow, cats take flight,
Chasing sunbeams, what a sight!
Frosty whiskers freeze in time,
While squirrels plot their sneaky crime.

A snowman winks, his carrot nose,
Wonders if he'll get new clothes.
Children giggle, slipping down,
While frost clings tight to every crown.

Penguins slide with playful grace,
On frozen ponds, a very funny place.
Snowflakes dance like they've had too much,
While boots get stuck; they lose the touch.

Laughter rings through trees so bright,
As nature dons her frosty white.
And in this whirl of winter fun,
Even icy hearts can run.

Candlelit Breezes

In the chilly air, candles sway,
As the frost tries to join the play.
A luminary's flicker, oh so bright,
It might just scare away the night.

Jackets tangled in the breeze,
As dogs compete to chase the leaves.
While timid curls of smoke do tease,
And everyone must duck with ease.

Hot cocoa mustache, with a laugh,
Spills over when you make a gaff.
A marshmallow lands on someone's nose,
And suddenly we all strike poses.

With laughter, we twirl, oh what a sight,
In the frosty air, everything's right.
Each glow and giggle breaks the dawn,
In a merry dance of frost and yawn.

A Canvas of Twinkling Frost

A canvas white, so sparkly neat,
The frosty grass feels like cold feet.
Snowflakes land, performing tricks,
While snowballs fly like magic flicks.

Yet there's a risk in every throw,
When cheeks go red from too much snow.
A snow angel lands with a squeal,
Then rolls away, oh what a deal!

Frosty fingers, they wave and shake,
As hot tea spills due to that break.
But who needs warmth when fun's at stake,
Let the frosty pranks awake!

A dance on ice, a quirky plight,
Each tumble brings a new delight.
In this bright world of chill and cheer,
Every frosty giggle is sincere.

Enchanted Glow of the Dawn

The sun peeks out, a playful tease,
Its warmth tricks trees with a gentle squeeze.
Puppies chase their tails in glee,
While birds wear hats, just wait and see.

With every step, a crunch and crack,
As we glide on paths of icy track.
A frosty palette, oh so surreal,
Yet everyone's having a hearty meal!

Mittens lost to the snowman's charm,
Who's giving hugs but causing harm.
Yet laughter spills as snowflakes fall,
And winter's mischief charms us all.

So let us dance through the morning light,
Embracing frosty joy and delight.
In this realm of ice and fun,
We find that winter's just begun.

Dawn's Embrace

The sun spills like cheese on toast,
Brightening the world, an early boast.
Chickens frolic, pecking for treats,
While I shiver in my warmest sheets.

Squirrels dance, wearing frosty caps,
Thinking they're cool with their winter laps.
The trees laugh, needles glistening bright,
As if saying, 'Look! We're a snowman's delight!'

My breath puffs out like a train's hot steam,
The world's a big playground, or so it seems.
But snowball fights turn my cheeks to red,
As I slip on ice and fall on my head!

So here's to mornings, crisp and keen,
Where all things sparkle, a festive scene.
With giggles and slips upon the lane,
Let's celebrate dawn like a champagne!

Winter's Glimmer

Sunrise tickles the chilly ground,
Icicles hang like a crystal crown.
The coffee pot splutters, what a tune,
While I'm lost in thoughts of warm afternoon.

Frosty windows foretell a funny day,
Where snowmen wink and kids laugh and play.
But my gloves are missing, no finger to spare,
I wear socks on my hands, what a silly flair!

The dog darts out, leaping with zeal,
While I'm bundled up like an onion meal.
Snowflakes dance like polka dots bright,
Making the world feel just right for a fight!

So bring on the giggles in winter's embrace,
With snowball battles and funny face race.
Each day is a joke wrapped in frost,
Let's savor the moments, never be lost!

Sun-Kissed Ice

The sun peeks out, a mischievous grin,
Melting the frost, let the fun begin.
Skaters wobble on makeshift rinks,
As ducks quack jokes over coffee drinks.

Pancakes are flipping, so fluffy and tall,
But I miss my mouth, and a syrupy fall.
The cat's on the ice, slipping with glee,
While I'm trying to focus, so full of spree!

Snow coats the trees in a fluffy white,
They sway and they giggle as day turns bright.
But I trip on a branch, oh what a show,
Like a clumsy dancer in a wintery flow!

With mugs of hot cocoa and laughter abound,
These mornings bring joy, so silly and round.
A toast to the chaos and icy delight,
Where every trip adds a laugh to the light!

Shimmering Breath of Daybreak

Dawn breaks and stretches, yawning wide,
While birds chirp songs from morning tide.
My toes are cold, a frozen retreat,
I dance like a penguin in mismatched feet.

The road is a mirror, reflecting the sun,
While I take a tumble—oh, wasn't that fun?
My neighbor chuckles, sipping his brew,
As I hop like a rabbit, feeling brand new!

Snowflakes tickle the nose with their flair,
While I chase my hat in the frosty air.
Every gust giggles, tickling my cheek,
Making me laugh till I can hardly speak!

So here's to the laughter wrapped in the chill,
With morning mischief and a wind that's a thrill.
Let's celebrate mornings that sparkle and cheer,
With funny little moments we'll hold ever dear!

A Tapestry of Ice and Gold

In winter's grip, the sun peeks out,
A squirrel slips, oh what a shout!
He slides on ice, in a furry dash,
While folks just sip their warming stash.

The trees are dressed in shimmering white,
As if the world is feeling quite light.
The postman slips and lands on his butt,
We all just laugh, what a funny rut!

The birds are chirping, hopping about,
Dancing in puddles, it's quite the clout.
They find their joy in the morning's chill,
With frosty feet, they frolic at will.

So raise a cup to this quirky spree,
Where laughter meets the icy glee.
In this tapestry of glint and grin,
Each day we twirl, let the fun begin!

Sunlight's Tender Caress

A ray slips through the window's line,
Awakens us with a goofy twine.
The cat stretches wide, makes a great flop,
As sunlight tickles, it surely pops!

The toast doth burn, but eggs do dance,
In this crazy morn, we take a chance.
With jam gone rogue and butter in flight,
Breakfast becomes a merry sight!

Outside the world wears a jeweled cloak,
While laughter erupts, oh what a joke!
Snowman's missing the carrot nose,
A cookie thief? Well, that's how it goes!

We sip our warmth with glee in each sip,
In sunlight's hug, we sharply flip.
With morning's antics so light and bright,
We treasure the laughter, our hearts take flight!

Morning's Frost-kissed Dazzle

The ground's a canvas, painted so sly,
With frosty fingers, the fog drifts by.
A dog runs wild, chasing its tail,
In a dance so silly, it tips like a whale!

Neighbors bundled in layers galore,
Shuffling about, then tripping once more.
A snowflake lands right on my nose,
And laughter erupts, oh how it grows!

The coffee spills, a hot little shock,
As we race outside, ready to mock.
With snowballs flying, a playful fight,
Who knew frost could bring such delight?

So here's to the morning that tickles our toes,
A time for good jests, where fun freely flows.
In frosty dazzle, we find our cheer,
Together we laugh, embracing good vibes here!

Crystalized Awakenings

Awake to sparkles on the spread lawn,
My slippers slip as I gracefully yawn.
A penguin in slippers? You're not far off,
With socks that sparkle, I twirl and scoff!

Hot cocoa spills like a chocolate rain,
A splash here and there; oh, what a gain!
Frothy mustaches on muggles so bright,
In this merry moment, it's quite the sight!

The kids bundle up for a snowball fight,
"More ammo, quick!" they shout in delight.
While parents just sit, sipping their brew,
They giggle and grin, just watching the crew!

So cheer for the mornings all crisp and clear,
With laughter and fun ringing in our ear.
In crystalized joy, we find a new start,
With smiles and humor that warm every heart!

A Tapestry of Frost and Glow

In the morning, I slip and slide,
My breath a cloud, my shoes untied.
The sun peeks out, a lazy grin,
Did I just see a squirrel spin?

With frost-kissed grass, we start to play,
Hats and mittens are all the way.
Snowmen wobble, their noses droop,
One fell over, now that's a scoop!

A shimmer here, a sparkle there,
Chasing shadows with madcap flair.
The air is brisk, but spirits rise,
As we dance like goofballs in disguise.

It's all a joke, this winter stuff,
But hot cocoa makes it less rough.
I'll take the freeze and silly sights,
For laughs abound on chilly nights.

Dappled Morning Magic

Waking up feels like a prank,
Pajamas damp; I swear they stank.
Outside the window, a frosty show,
A dance of flakes, all in a row.

I step outside, a snowflake wig,
Trying hard to not do a jig.
Each breath I take fogs up the view,
Like a dragon, blowing burps anew.

Nature giggles, it's quite the tease,
With frosty air that bites and frees.
To build a snowman takes some skill,
But falling down? Now that's a thrill!

Oh, winter's laugh is crisp and bright,
It jokes with me 'til late at night.
A magic spell of ice and fun,
With every giggle, the day's just begun!

Chasing Light Through Frost

Morning stroll on a slippery lane,
I slip and slide like I've lost my brain.
The sun is peeking, a playful tease,
As I chase light with frozen knees.

The trees wear coats of sparkling white,
Their branches wear hats, what a silly sight!
I spot a bird, it's wearing a scarf,
Laughing out loud, oh, how I laugh!

Chasing shadows that jump and play,
My nose turns red, but that's okay.
If I fall down, I'll just roll like a ball,
In this frosty fun, I can't help but sprawl.

With giggles echoing through the air,
And winter's charm beyond compare.
I tip my hat to the frosty chill,
Life's a joke, and I'm here for the thrill!

Glimmering Chills

Frosty breath and goosebumps dance,
Just one wrong step and I lose my pants.
The pavement glimmers like a mirror bright,
Guess what? I'm skating! What a sight!

Hot chocolate's steaming, my hands are cold,
But who needs gloves when you've got bold?
The wind whooshes, it gives me a shove,
I wobble around like a clumsy dove.

In the sparkling sun, I hear a cheer,
As a snowball whizzes right past my ear.
My friends unite for a playful fight,
This chilly day is pure delight!

So here we are, in a frosty chase,
Warming hearts in a goofy race.
With laughter echoing through the chills,
This silly winter gives us all the thrills!

Bright Hues on a Chilly Canvas

The sun peeks out with a cheeky grin,
Warming up the snow like it's a cousin kin.
Frosted edges, they start to drip,
While squirrels plan their acorn trip.

A rabbit hops in a top hat so bright,
Dancing around in sheer delight.
"Come join the party!" he seems to say,
While ice skates twirl in frosty play.

Kids with snowballs, a fake snow fight,
Throwing snowflakes with all their might.
Laughter erupts, a wintery cheer,
As snowmen wobble with no sense of fear.

So gather round this colorful scene,
With hot cocoa and marshmallows obscene.
Each chilly day paints a warm delight,
In this whimsical world of winter's light.

Whispered Lucence

The sun's a prankster at dawn's first peek,
Wrapping trees in a shiny, frosty cheek.
"Good morning, world!" it cheerily beams,
While birds sing loud in fractured dreams.

Ice on branches like nature's bling,
A quirky dance that makes hearts sing.
But don't slip now, that patch is slick,
You might just end up doing a trick!

Penguins slide fast on the frozen lake,
Cheeky faces, they just can't take.
Wobbling about, they lose their grace,
In a frosty race, it's a silly chase.

So let the chuckles take their flight,
Through crisp air and morning light.
Winter brings laughter, bright and clear,
With frosted fun that we all endear.

Translucent Gleams Amidst the Freeze

Sunshine glimmers like a playful cat,
Creeping on rooftops, like "What's up, brat?"
Snowflakes shimmy as they drift down slow,
Like tiny dancers in a winter show.

Frosty breath escapes like a cloud,
While neighbors gossip, all bundled and proud.
"Did you see me? I'm quite the sight,"
In winter coats, they clamber and fight.

Hot soup simmers like a bubbling cheer,
While snowflakes tickle kids' faces near.
Sleds zoom by, a thrilling craze,
As laughter echoes in winter's maze.

With every twinkle, there's joy in cold,
As stories of comfort and warmth unfold.
In the land of frost, oh what a tease,
Nature's comedy brings us to our knees.

Glows of Solitude

The sun is shy, just peeking through,
It blushes softly, as if it knew.
Trees in their coats, all frosted and neat,
Dance with the wind, keeping the beat.

A cat saunters in its warm fur coat,
Pretending to be a mighty boat.
With paws in the snow, it looks for fun,
In the shimmering world, basking in sun.

Snowflakes catch noses, stick like glue,
Making faces funny, and spirits anew.
Whispers of winter in shades of white,
As giggles sparkle in morning light.

So embrace the chill, with laughter loud,
In this frosty world, we all feel proud.
For moments shared in a snowy expanse,
Bring forth the joy in a wintry dance.

Chasing Shadows in Mist

In the dawn's embrace, I dance with glee,
My own shadow laughs, what's wrong with me?
Slipping on ice, a friend I might chase,
But all I catch is my own silly face.

With mist in the air, I jest and I spin,
Snowflakes like confetti come tumbling in.
I pirouette wildly, then stumble and fall,
A snowball lands right on my nose, what a call!

Warm Glows on Winter's Breath

The sun peeks through clouds, a soft golden grin,
I toast my hands, but they swat at the wind.
A squirrel runs by, wearing snow as a hat,
He stops for a moment, then scolds like a brat.

With hot cocoa spills, I laugh at my shirt,
The steam from my mug looks like a small flirt.
Snowmen are frowning, their noses askew,
I'll make them a scarf from my woolly shoe.

Ethereal Frost

The frost on the window, a masterpiece drawn,
I trace it with fingers, till it's all gone.
Outside the cats play, they prance and they pounce,
But slip on their tails, oh how they can bounce!

I sip on my tea, it's tastier hot,
Yet every few sips, I'm forgot and I'll rot.
My friends give me hugs, but oh what a sight,
We all freeze together with giggles and light!

The Light Between the Chill

In the middle of winter, the sun's got a wink,
I twirl like a ballerina, but spill my drink.
With laughter I tumble, I roll in the snow,
A snow angel's case for a hot cocoa flow.

The shadows are laughing, they tickle my toes,
While icicles dangle like pointy bad prose.
So let's all be goofy, it's fun as can be,
With sparkles of frost, we'll be silly and free.

Twinkling Frost on the Grass

Tiny sparkles dance at dawn,
A chilly carpet stretches on.
Socks on hands, how funny they look,
While nibbling on a frost-kissed nook.

Sneaky shivers, what a sight,
Sneezing snowflakes feel just right.
I swear my nose could freeze and pop,
As I hop like a bouncy top!

Hiccups from the icy air,
Each giggle bites, without a care.
I chase my breath like a lost kite,
Cackling loud—what pure delight!

All around, a silvery glow,
As clumsy squirrels put on a show.
We're stumbling, sliding, what a blast,
With every frosty slip—make it last!

Resplendent Chill

Morning whispers with a sneeze,
Check your nose, it's quite the breeze!
I wear my scarf like a fancy chef,
Looking puffed, my winter prep!

Frosty windows, funny faces,
I draw a wiggly smile in places.
The world is chilly, but don't you pout,
Dance like penguins, there's joy about!

Hot cocoa spills on my new coat,
Oh no, that's not how I planned to float!
With laughter echoing through the trees,
This frozen madness puts me at ease.

Snowmen wobble as they glisten,
I swear that one just tried to listen!
With frosty wigs made of spun sugar,
We laugh till our tummies begin to tigger!

Shimmering Silence at Sunrise

In the stillness, there's a giggle,
The sun's a jester making us wiggle.
A frosty breath warms up the day,
While my boots squeak, what can I say?

Trees wearing their glistening crowns,
As I wear mismatched winter gowns.
Panic at the snowball fight,
I duck too late, it's in my sight!

I see my shadow sliding away,
Sprinting fast, who will win today?
The breeze tickles my funny bone,
As I trip over my snowy throne.

Squirrels laugh, plotting their heist,
Nabbing my snacks—oh, isn't that nice?
With every tumble, my heart does leap,
As we roll in snow, giggling deep!

Gleaming Paths in Winter's Grasp

Paths aglow with icy splendor,
Ice-skating squirrels, oh what a contender!
I chase my hat that danced away,
And stumbled loudly—what a ballet!

Neighbors glued to windows wide,
While I ride my sled down snowed-up slides.
Who knew that falling could be so grand?
While giggling snowflakes dashed from hand to hand!

North winds shush in a playful tease,
My cheeks are pink, they aim to freeze.
The trees chuckle in their quiet stance,
As I woefully attempt to prance!

Wondrous glitters on every pine,
Creating mischief, oh how divine!
With every slip we find a cheer,
This winter waltz fills hearts with beer!

Radiant Morningsweet

The sun awakes with a wink,
Warming the toe of my socked foot.
I stumble out to the kitchen sink,
Where yesterday's coffee lies resolute.

A dance of shadows prances bright,
As I jiggle through half-open blinds.
The cat gives me a judging sight,
While contemplating the loaf that binds.

Waffles or pancakes, what will it be?
The fridge offers its chilly embrace.
Maybe just cereal, quite carefree,
And a splash of milk spills in the race!

Filtered Glimmers of the Day

Oh look, a shimmer on the ground,
A rogue ice cube lost its way,
My footsteps echo a funny sound,
As I slip in a slip-and-slide ballet.

The neighbors peer from behind a tree,
With coffee mugs raised in cheers.
"Is he okay, or just fancy-free?"
They giggle loud, as laughter nears.

Birds tweet gossip, calling my name,
While squirrels plot a nutty scheme.
I'm a star in their morning game,
With mismatched socks, I'm their wild dream.

Brilliant Frost-laced Echoes

Frosty panes reveal my breath,
Like a dragon warming its lair.
I wave to the trees, as if they're my pets,
That shiver and shake in the frosty air.

The mailbox creaks with icy pride,
A letter from Aunt Gertrude awaits.
"Please don't wear snow boots when you slide,"
She warns me, which is just great!

With a marshmallow hat, I prepare for the fun,
As blizzards paint my witty face.
I'll ride on my sled till the day is done,
Then come in and eat all the food in the place!

Warmth Thawing the Chill

A cup of cocoa in hand, I trot,
Finding solace from the cold wind's bite.
Whipped cream mountains, the perfect lot,
Oh, how marshmallows soar in delight!

I wear a scarf that's two sizes too big,
Wrapped up like a burrito in style.
I lounge like a king with a toothpaste wig,
As I plan my next frosty-filed mile.

Laughter bubbles from toasty hearts,
As snowflakes start to dance and twirl.
With sledding and laughing, the day imparts,
A winter wonder, a joyous whirl!

Morning's Gentle Glow

Dew drops sparkle, sunlight's tease,
The cat jumps high, lands in the breeze.
Coffee brews in a clumsy way,
A dance of spills to start the day.

Out on the porch, socks on the lawn,
Birds shout secrets, the neighbor's gone.
A squirrel winks, as if in jest,
Chasing his tail, he's doing his best.

Pancakes flip, they soar in flight,
A syrup river, a sticky sight.
The dog chases shadows on the wall,
While I just hope not to take a fall.

With laughter bright and smiles so wide,
The silly moments we cannot hide.
Mornings crackle with fun galore,
As we tumble through this kitchen door.

Whispering Chills

Jack Frost nips at my silly nose,
Wearing mittens with holes, goodness knows.
Slipping and sliding on icy ground,
The penguin walk is the new cool found.

Tea steams up, a comforting sight,
But watch those marshmallows take to flight!
They bounce and float, a fluffy crew,
Landing splat in the brew, oh boo!

Scarves wrapped tight like mummies unseen,
While my hat's spinning like a washing machine.
Fingers frozen, they wave like a wand,
Summoning warmth, of which I am fond.

Giggles echo in the crisp, cold air,
Each frosty breath a whimsical flair.
Oh, the chill comes with such a thrill,
In winter's playful, joyful spill.

Frosted Reverie

Morning fog like a fluffy cloak,
A snowman grins—did he just poke?
I step outside with a leap and a bound,
But oh! My foot slips, I topple down.

Puffy jackets, a fashion spree,
Hats askew like they're trying to flee.
Children giggle in snowball fights,
While I dodge, trying not to take bites.

The crunch of snow, like crispy chips,
I dance along with flopping quips.
A snow angel forms, but I'm stuck instead,
A snowman wannabe, fully outspread.

As sunlight beams through the frosty layers,
I laugh at the fun, what brilliant players!
Winter's charm brings its own delight,
In every flake, oh what a sight!

The Dance of Light and Ice

Sunrise stumbles, a sleepy dance,
While ice cubes clink, giving me a chance.
The kettle whistles a hot, silly tune,
As I juggle muffins, oh, what a boon!

Chilly winds play peek-a-boo,
Hats fly off, a scarf bid adieu.
A neighbor chuckles as I chase after,
The playful wind, a giggly laughter.

Frosty windows with doodles and cheer,
I swear my coffee's in on up here.
It swirls and dives, a caffeinated show,
While I sip slowly, oh where did it go?

Each morning unfolds, a quirky delight,
With silly adventures, laughter in sight.
Let's embrace the cold, let our spirits lift,
In the dance where warmth and frost merrily shift.

The Shimmer of a New Day

A sunbeam slips on socks askew,
Awakening the world anew.
Coffee's brewing, pot on the run,
Stirring dreams of warmth and fun.

Waking just to chase our breath,
Laughing through the morning's heft.
Chasing shadows, ducks take flight,
Who knew frost could feel so light?

Chattering squirrels throw their cheer,
While frost makes all the giggles near.
Snowflakes dance like they're in a race,
Who knew mornings could hold such grace?

The fluff on tops of hats they wiggle,
While pine trees lose their frosty giggle.
A day of warmth and frosty delight,
Bringing laughter till the night.

Morning's Radiant Breath

Crisp is the air where aromas blend,
With pancakes flipping, oh what a trend!
Maple syrup starts to flow,
Dancing on the plates like a show.

Frogs on the pond wear winter wear,
Jumping with laughter without a care.
The breakfast table fills with cheer,
Who knew mornings could bring such beer?

Toast pops up in grand array,
Butter slips and tries to play.
Squeaky chairs join in the fun,
As laughter mingles with the sun.

With mittens lost and giggles spread,
Chasing whirlwinds with warmth ahead.
Here's to mornings, drowsy yet bright,
Bringing joy and no hint of fright.

Luminescent Winter Whispers

Pillow fights with frosty breath,
Tell tales of warmth, defy all myths.
As clouds play peek-a-boo in the sky,
We laugh so hard that we might cry.

Socks are mismatched, a dreadful sight,
But who cares when the sun shines bright?
Snow angels giggle in pure delight,
While raccoons steal snacks from the night.

Bouncing bunnies hop with glee,
In the frost, they do agree.
Hot cocoa, marshmallows float and dive,
Who needs sleep? We're truly alive!

Slippers dance on chilly floors,
As we slam open the creaky doors.
Whispers of joy in the morning glow,
Making funny memories to bestow.

Flashes of Warmth on Chilled Ground

In the garden, giggles sprout,
With snowflakes laughing all about.
Hot chocolate dreams and squeaky toys,
Caught in breezes, oh what joys!

Sunburnt cheeks from frosty pranks,
Sleds zoom past with gleeful thanks.
Cats in coats, they prance and play,
Who knew they'd love this chill today?

Sunbeams dance on icy streams,
Where every splash is full of dreams.
Skates glide over laughter's tune,
As winter's chill becomes our boon.

So let's bundle up, romp around,
With warmth that glows beneath the ground.
Every moment is a playful swap,
In the joy where frosty winters hop!

Sparkling Reflections on Ice

The pond wears a shiny glaze,
The ducks glide in dreamy daze.
Ice skaters slip, they giggle and fall,
Pajamas on, they give it their all.

Laughter echoes through the trees,
As snowflakes dance on a brisk breeze.
A snowman topples, a carrot flies,
The neighbors chuckle, what a surprise!

Sunshine winks off icy strands,
While kids make castles in winter sands.
Hot cocoa spills, what a messy sight,
When marshmallows bounce in pure delight!

With every tumble and every cheer,
Winter shenanigans draw us near.
We'll treasure these moments, laughter's freeze,
As fun floats on frosted seas!

Frost's Light Harness

The chill wraps us like a silly hug,
Woolly sweaters — oh, what a snug!
Frost draws art on every window,
  It's winter's doodle, let it flow!

Hats like muffins, scattered about,
Snowflakes fall, we jump and shout.
Sleds go flying, catching the sun,
Wipeouts are best, they're all in good fun!

The ground sparkles like a disco ball,
Jokes take flight, we're having a ball.
With every sneeze, we giggle aloud,
  Winter's antics, we're truly proud!

When ice cream cones turn into slush,
We take quick bites in a frosty rush.
Happiness wrapped in every laugh,
  In the chill, we found our craft!

Celestial Hues of Chilly Morn

Mornings break with a frosty grin,
As slippers slide and joy begins.
A cat sprawls on the window's frost,
In this cozy world, we're never lost.

The sky wears clouds, a cotton candy hue,
While socks miss their match, oh, what a view!
Breath fogs gently, like whispers of fun,
As we chase the laughter, a blazing run!

A trio of birds in a frosty line,
Attempt a song but then just whine.
It seems the chill has robbed their tune,
Yet still they chirp under the moon!

Hands in pockets, we march outside,
With snowballs prepared, it's time to collide!
In this wintry scene, we find such glee,
With chuckles galore, all wild and free!

Wandering Through Dappled Frost

The grass glistens like it's sprinkled with sugar,
And boots crunch softly like a sleepy juggler.
With every step, a frosty crunch,
We laugh like kids, oh, what a bunch!

Tangled up in scarves, we roam,
Chasing snowflakes that feel like home.
A snowball fight breaks out with zeal,
Who knew cold clutter could feel so real?

Frosty plants wear hats from the night,
While squirrels gather, not quite polite.
Pine cones scatter, a raucous scene,
It's a winter party, we reign supreme!

With cheeks aglow and spirits bright,
We twirl and spin in sheer delight.
In this chilly wonder, we share our smiles,
As frosty laughter warms the miles!

Glacial Dawn

The sun peeks out with a giggle,
As snowflakes dance, a frosty wiggle.
Birds are chirping, but they are cold,
Fluffy sweaters they wish to hold.

Snowmen in hats are having fun,
With carrot noses, they start to run.
They slip and slide on the shiny ice,
Chasing their dreams, oh, isn't this nice?

Ducks wearing earmuffs, oh what a sight,
Sipping hot cocoa, they feel just right.
They quack a tune, it's quite the show,
On chilly mornings, their talents glow.

Boots squeak as we tread through the land,
Making snow angels, isn't it grand?
Laughter echoes through the crisp air,
Winter's surprise, beyond compare.

Amber Hues on Snow

Morning drops in with a wink,
Lighting the world, causing us to think.
Bunnies hop in warm, fuzzy socks,
While squirrels parade in their winter frocks.

Snowmen gossip, sipping their soup,
Talking of snowball fights and who's in the loop.
Children bundle, ready to play,
As parents hold coffee, just trying to stay.

Candies droop from the trees, what a tease,
A sweet wonderland that's sure to please.
Nature giggles with a fun little twist,
With vibrant colors that can't be missed.

Sunshine winks, giving warm hugs,
As critters dance, doing their jugs.
In frozen moments, joy never flakes,
With amber hues, the laughter breaks.

Cool Sunbeams

The sunlight stretches with a yawn,
Waking the world, greeting the dawn.
A cat in a hat, looking quite sassy,
As puppies prance, feeling all classy.

Shadows play tricks on silly feet,
As kids stumble over a snowball fleet.
Giggles erupt, the fun never ends,
In icy realms where the chill transcends.

A snow globe shakes with a merry shake,
Inside, a dance that causes a quake.
Cool beams tease the frost, letting it twirl,
As laughing flakes decide to unfurl.

With cheeks that glow and noses bright,
Frosty mornings feel just right.
As snowflakes glitter, merry and bold,
We chase after joy, because life's gold.

Luminous Frost

Frosty patterns make us pause,
Nature creates with many applause.
Chasing rabbits in coats of white,
Squeaky shoes add to the delight.

Icicles dangle, a shimmering tease,
Snowball fights that bring us to our knees.
Laughter erupts with each playful throw,
On winter's canvas, we steal the show.

Hot chocolate bubbles, the scent in the air,
As marshmallows float without a care.
A dance with penguins, their waddle so slick,
While kids race by on sleds, oh so quick.

As twilight falls with a wink and a nudge,
Nature's sparkle, we simply won't budge.
Each frosty morn's a treasure to boast,
In this winter circus, we're loving the most.

Glistening Echoes of Morning

In the dawn's soft embrace, jokes unfold,
Sunbeams play tag, oh, so bold.
A giggle escapes from the frost-bitten trees,
As squirrels chase shadows, full of mischief and tease.

Pajamas all frozen, stuck to my thighs,
Coffee's my armor; I wake with a sigh.
Birds chirp like they're cracking a code,
While ice on the window frames a glittering load.

Slippers are slipping, it's quite a ballet,
I dance with the frost as I fumble my way.
A snowman's grin beams from the yard,
Wishing for warmth, but life's just a shard.

So here in the morn where the giggles collide,
With lightheartedness swirling like a snowy slide.
Embrace the chill, it's a laugh, I insist,
Frosty adventures can never be missed!

Sunlit Crystals

With diamonds twinkling on every branch,
I'm here in my coat, doing the frost dance.
Ice cubes refuse to stay in my drink,
They're shivering too, I swear, just think!

Carrots for noses in the whirling snow,
I slip on a patch, oh no, here I go!
Laughter erupts, as I land with a 'thud',
Perfecting my role in this glittery flood.

Neighbors peek out, it's a frosty parade,
Hot chocolate flows in a sweet escapade.
A snowball flies, oh, the joy we create,
Frosty mornings make snowmen first-rate!

So join in the fun, with a smile full of glee,
In this winter wonder, there's laughter, you see.
Glistening crystals invite us to play,
What a crazy beginning to another cold day!

Morning's Embered Breath

Mornings arrive in a puff of white mist,
Where snowflakes and giggles can't be dismissed.
I trip on my laces, the world's upside down,
While snowflakes join in, they giggle and frown.

Yet warmth finds a way through my small window pane,
As sunshine peeks in, it's playing the game.
It tickles the shadows, brings forth a cheer,
In the chill of the morn, hit snooze—never fear!

The kettle is whistling, it sounds like a song,
As pancakes flip over, I hope I'm not wrong.
In syrupy splashes, morning grins wide,
With buttered up pancakes, the best source of pride!

So let's laugh at the frost and toast to our fate,
Ember-like mornings that never feel late.
With a cup in my hand, I'll conquer the day,
In this crisp snowy world, let's frolic and play!

Icicles of Light

Down from the eaves, they dangle and sway,
Icicles glimmer like stars in the day.
My nose is frozen, but the giggles are bright,
Joyful banter drifts up in the light.

Who knew the snowmen were quite such a crew?
They gossip and laugh, have a tea party too.
With each icy drip, they share all their tales,
While hitching a ride on the frosty gales.

There's a cartwheel of sunlight, spinning around,
Making glistening circles upon the cold ground.
The snowflakes misbehave, twirling in loops,
While warm smiles emerge from quiet little groups.

So let's raise a cheer, for the chill in the air,
As ice sculptures chuckle, with nary a care.
In this whimsical morning, so silly and bright,
We dance with the frost, in the icicles' light!

Dappled Light on Frosty Fields

The sun pokes out, what a sight,
Chasing away the chill of night.
My breath is a cloud, puffs of white,
'Tis not my coffee, just morning's bite!

Squirrels scurry with nuts in tow,
In icy armor, they prance like pros.
They slip and slide, oh how they throw
Their little acorns in joyous throws!

The crunch of grass under my feet,
Winter's fairies throw snowball treats.
I toss one high, it's quite the feat,
Missed the squirrel, he made a retreat!

Now the sun dances on frozen streams,
While I try to catch snowflakes in dreams.
Watch out for the puddles, it seems,
Splish splash! My socks are soaking themes!

Auroras of the Morning

Morning comes with a flicker and flash,
Like my neighbor's cat, ready to dash.
Colors swirling like a painter's stash,
Yet here I sit, with my cereal crash.

A wink from the dawn, oh what a tease,
Crisp air tickles, brings me to my knees.
Coffee brews as the sunlight frees,
And I may just trip on a pile of leaves!

Chasing the glow with mismatched socks,
Fashion icon? Or am I a fox?
I slip on ice, give it solid knocks,
More like a mermaid, in a pond of rocks!

Dancing shadows play tricks on the ground,
The sky laughs, with skies so profound.
My cat's plotting—she's the queen unbound,
Ready to pounce, with her stealthy sound!

Serene Ember Mauves

The hues of dawn, a blend so bright,
While I fumble with my blanket tight.
My hair's a mess, just not quite right,
Like a raccoon dressing for a concert night!

Morning giggles, the birds chime in,
As I try hard not to trip on my chin.
Fumble for toast, and guess what? Win!
It's stuck to the plate, but I dive right in!

The frost on grass glistens, a show,
I slip on a patch, feeling quite low.
But laughter erupts as I spin like a pro,
And the neighbors all cheer at my fresh ballet flow!

With every color that dances and glows,
I bundle up tight against chilly blows.
But grinning from ear to ear, as it goes,
This day's got potential—even with frosty toes!

Radiant Shivers

Chilled air bites as I step outside,
Underneath my scarf, I'm trying to hide.
My nose runs freely, can't keep it tied,
Just a wild-pool of laughter, oh what a ride!

The sun sneezes gold, just hits the right cake,
While I'm doing the penguin to avoid a mistake.
Snowflakes spiral like stars on a lake,
I catch one on my tongue—what a fun break!

A snowman calls, 'Come build, come play!'
With hands like flippers, I create him today.
He topples over, much to my dismay,
Sports all around, in a frosty ballet!

Amidst all the shivers, I'm snug and alive,
With giggles and snorts, we all closely strive.
The morning's a show, not just to survive,
Who knew icy delights would help me thrive?

Frosted Radiance

A sunny sneeze at dawn's bright call,
The icy breath makes snowflakes fall.
With mittens lost and socks askew,
I trip on dreams, oh what a view!

The chilly air, a joker's tease,
My nose is red, but I feel the breeze.
The frosty ground, a slippery ride,
I slide along with laughter wide.

Carrots dance in frosty mayhem,
While snowmen don a hat from them.
A cheeky rabbit hops with glee,
As we sip cocoa, warm and free.

Each sparkling breath a frosty jest,
Though winter's chill puts us to test.
With giggles shared, we shake and shake,
Let's laugh at winter's grand snowflake!

Light's Frosted Embrace

Morning giggles greet the freeze,
While icicles dangle like frozen tease.
I slipped a bit, oh what a sight,
The dog just laughed with pure delight!

Sunbeams poke through icy glass,
The curtains ripple, oh what sass!
I swear that snowman winked at me,
With a carrot nose, such mystery!

The air crisp like grandma's quilt,
I wrapped my buns, oh how they wilt!
A frosty kiss from Jack, so bold,
Wrapped in warmth, we're never cold!

The world a stage of sparkly beams,
Where snowballs soar like our wild dreams.
Let's catch each laugh, a snowy fling,
In this embrace, let our joy spring!

Frost and Ember Dance

At dawn, the world twirls in white,
Snowflakes giggle, what a sight!
Frosty fingers play on my nose,
Like playful elves in winter's clothes.

Chasing shadows, slipping fast,
Where laughter flies and moments last.
A tumble here, a frosty roll,
Warming hearts with joy, our goal!

Beneath the branches, winter's song,
A frosty ballet, oh so strong.
With chatter bright and spirits high,
We weave our way through the frosty sky.

Embers crackle, the fire's embrace,
We dance around, oh what a chase!
With cocoa cups and merry cheer,
Let's twirl away the winter fear!

Glinting Dreams at Daybreak

From slumber deep to morning's cheer,
The world awakes, what's that I hear?
A clatter here, a coffee spill,
With dreams of snow and winter thrill.

My breath a puff of frosty mist,
I juggle dreams, oh what a twist!
The sun shines bright, it winks at me,
Snowflakes pirouette, wild and free!

With snowy clothes and silly hats,
I stumble 'round just like the cats.
The meadow blinks in glinting white,
Is that a snowman? Oh, what a sight!

As laughter fills the chilly air,
We launch ourselves, with frosty flair.
With each bright smile and silly game,
We greet the day, unashamedly lame!

The Heat of a Chilly Morning

Under blankets I lay with glee,
Hoping for warmth and some coffee.
Outside the world's frozen, quite absurd,
I'm dreaming of sun, that's the word!

My socks mismatched, a fashion thrill,
With fuzzy slippers that give a chill.
My breath is fog, a ghostly sight,
I laugh out loud, what a winter's night!

The cat by the heater, king of the room,
Is plotting a coup, oh what a gloom!
He gives me a glare, in his comfy lair,
"Are you really awake? You must be quite rare!"

But here's to the fun in this frostbite dance,
Where every snowflake gives nature a chance.
So pour some hot cocoa, and let's all embrace,
This chilly chaos, a warm-hearted race!

Glows of a Winter's Rise

The dawn peeks in with a wink and a smile,
While I yawn like a bear, can't quite wake for a while.
Mistakes can be made in a sleepy haze,
Like mistaking a sweater for a shirt on a craze!

Outside my window, the world wears a cape,
Of silvery frost, a wintertime drape.
Birds are chirping, they sing so loud,
While I wrap up tight, like a burrito proud!

I see my neighbor, slipping on ice,
With snacks in his pockets, oh, so nice.
Down he goes, in a flurry of snow,
But up he springs, with a laugh and a glow!

So here's to the beauty, and laughter it brings,
In cozy old sweaters and goofy old things.
Each glimmer and giggle on this bright winter morn,
Makes memories shine, like a bright little horn!

Crystal Sunlight

The sunlight dances on frosted trees,
While I stumble around, still half asleep, please.
In pajamas of plaid, I strut with pride,
Feeling quite fancy, in this snowy ride!

Icicles hang like a crystal parade,
I wonder if they'd like a lemonade?
With a splash and a giggle, they tinkle and chime,
While I waddle outside, committing a crime!

Snowballs are flying, laughter ensues,
As I duck from a snowman with mismatched shoes.
Friends gather round for a snowball fight,
Who knew winter could be so delightfully bright?

So here's to the mornings that frolic and shine,
Where fun is the rule, and all's mighty fine.
With coffee in hand, and warmth in our toes,
We embrace every minute, that's how the day goes!

Awakening in Chill

The alarm clock blares with a frosty shout,
I hit snooze once more, without a doubt.
Outside, the squirrels are dressed for a spree,
While I fumble to find my legs, oh, whee!

The toast pops up like a golden surprise,
But I forgot the jam, oh dear, what a prize.
A burly snowman is waiting outside,
With a carrot for nose, looking filled with pride!

Off to work, but oh, what a test,
With frozen fingers, I must dress my best.
A hat here, a scarf there, looking quite fine,
But I trip on a snowdrift, oh, how divine!

We'll laugh through the elements, that's our true style,
With frosted eyelashes and nose that's a mile.
So let's toast with hot chocolate, my warm fuzzy friend,
As we celebrate winter, until the very end!

Vivid Feathers of Frost

In the yard, birds wear coats,
Wobbling like they're riding boats.
Snowflakes land on noses red,
Silly sneezes fill their head.

Pigeons strut with winter flair,
Twirling round without a care.
Chasing snowflakes, oh what fun,
Their flapping makes them look like spun.

Glistening Threads of Dawn

A squirrel slips upon the ice,
Wobbling 'round, not thinking twice.
His acorn drops, he gives a shout,
Rolling off, he's knocked right out.

The sunlight brings a giggling grin,
As chilly winds play tag with chin.
With coffee cups and frosty toes,
We laugh aloud at how it goes.

Shards of Radiance

Sunbeams dance on tiny floors,
Predicament for those outdoors.
A snowball throw leads to surprise,
Covered heads and frosty eyes.

The shimmer sparkles on the ground,
With every crunch, a silly sound.
When friends slip, each gives a cheer,
Winter antics draw us near.

Sunlit Frosted Dreams

A dog leaps high, then falls flat,
Rolling down, it looks like that!
Winter coats and fuzzy hats,
Cuddly critters, playful spats.

Chasing shadows, they all race,
Laughter echoed, purest grace.
Picnic plans turn into slips,
We chuckle hard, it's on our lips.

Milton Keynes UK
Ingram Content Group UK Ltd.
UKHW020045271124
451585UK00012B/1064